D0130919

921 REV

Randolph, Ryan P.
Paul Revere and the
Minutemen of the American

	DATE DUE		

Siskiyou County
Office of Education Library
609 South Gold Street
Yreka, CA 96097

T 80160

THE LIBRARY OF
AMERICAN
LIVES AND TIMES™

PAUL REVERE

and the Minutemen of the American Revolution

Ryan P. Randolph

The Rosen Publishing Group's
PowerPlus Books™
New York

To Jo, with love,
for her patience and her confidence in me

Published in 2002 by The Rosen Publishing Group, Inc.
29 East 21st Street, New York, NY 10010

Copyright © 2002 by The Rosen Publishing Group, Inc.

All rights reserved. No part of this book may be reproduced in any form
without permission in writing from the publisher, except by a reviewer.

First Edition

Editor's Note: All quotations have been reproduced as they appeared in the let-
ters and diaries from which they were borrowed. No correction was made to
the inconsistent spelling that was common in that time period.

Library of Congress Cataloging-in-Publication Data

Randolph, Ryan P.
Paul Revere and the Minutemen of the American Revolution / author,
Ryan P. Randolph .
p. cm. — (The library of American lives and times) Includes bibliographical
references and index.
  ISBN 0–8239–5727–6 (alk. paper)
1. Revere, Paul, 1735–1818—Juvenile literature. 2. Statesmen—
Massachusetts—Biography—Juvenile literature. 3. Massachusetts—
History—Revolution, 1775–1783—Juvenile literature. 4. Lexington, Battle
of, 1775—Juvenile literature. 5. Concord, Battle of, 1775—Juvenile
literature. 6. Minutemen (Militia)—Massachusetts—Juvenile literature.
[1. Revere, Paul, 1735–1818. 2. Statesmen. 3. Silversmiths.
4. Massachusetts—History—Revolution, 1775–1783—Biography. 5. United
States—History—Revolution, 1775–1783—Biography.] I. Title. II. Series.
  F69.R43 R36 2001
  973.3'311'092—dc21

                                                              00–012978

Manufactured in the United States of America

CONTENTS

1. Paul Revere and the American Revolution

Paul Revere is best known to Americans for his midnight ride to Lexington during the night of April 18 and early morning of April 19 in 1775. Revere spread the word to the minutemen of New England that the British army was marching from Boston to Lexington and Concord.

As tensions between the colonies and the British government mounted, fear of conflict grew. Paul Revere and other American patriots developed what may be called an advance alarm system to warn the various towns outside of Boston if the British army was heading toward them. Each town spread the word to the next, and each town mobilized its militias. These militias, or citizen soldiers, had selected groups of minutemen who were trained to be ready at a moment's notice. The advance warning provided by Revere and other express

Opposite: This well-known oil painting of Paul Revere was painted by John Singleton Copley around 1768. Rather than showing Paul Revere in fine clothes as is traditionally done in portraits, Copley has captured an artisan in his natural setting. This painting reflects the simplicity of Revere's life and his pride in his work.

alarm riders allowed the minutemen time to get ready to face the British army at Lexington and at Concord.

The various running battles fought between the minutemen and the British army on April 19, 1775, are known together as the Battle of Lexington and Concord. These battles were the first open fighting between the British regular army and the minutemen and citizens of the colonies. More importantly, these were the first battles in the war that would lead to American independence from Britain and the beginning of the United States.

Paul Revere was not as important during the actual fighting of the American Revolution as he was in the events leading up to it. He did not gain status outside of Boston as a legendary patriot until 1862, nearly 90 years after his midnight ride. At this time, the celebrated poet Henry Wadsworth Longfellow wrote the famous poem that made Paul Revere a legend.

During his lifetime, Paul Revere was known for more than just his midnight ride. Before the beginning of the American Revolution, Paul Revere was a respected artisan known as a goldsmith. Artisans or mechanics, as they were known, were craftsmen who worked as carpenters, tailors, and shipbuilders,

---

This is a map of the east coast of America from 1780. The city highlighted in pink is Boston, and the city colored blue is Philadelphia. Paul Revere and other express riders brought news between the leaders in the two cities throughout the war.

among other occupations. Although called a goldsmith, Revere mostly worked with silver, and only sometimes with gold. He also had other side projects, such as engraving and the fitting and production of false teeth!

Before the outbreak of the Revolution, Revere was also an active patriot who was heavily involved in many political groups, such as the Sons of Liberty and the Masons. Even before his famous ride, Revere had already made several journeys to deliver news and messages between the leaders in Boston and the Continental Congresses in Philadelphia, as well as to bring news to places such as New York, Connecticut, and New Hampshire.

After the American Revolution, Paul Revere remained active in local government and politics. He organized fellow Boston mechanics in support of the new Federal Constitution, and helped to establish the Massachusetts Charitable Mechanics Association. This group looked after the rights of craftsmen and cared for members who had become sick or injured.

Paul Revere's main focus returned to his business life after the Revolution. With his sons to help in the silver shop, Revere focused more of his time on other businesses. He opened a hardware store for a short time. Then he started a foundry that made metal nails, spikes, and other materials for building ships. Revere also became known for high-quality church bells that he produced at his foundry. These bells still hang in churches in New England today.

In his later years, Revere began the first successful mill in America to specialize in rolling copper. Revere's new mill provided sheets of copper used to cover the bottoms of ships for the new American navy. Rolled copper from Revere's mill also covered the original dome of the Massachusetts statehouse.

From his silver, to his active involvement in pre-Revolutionary Boston politics, to his post-revolutionary business ventures, Paul Revere was an important individual for more than just his midnight ride. The life and times of Paul Revere exemplify what life was like in New England and America before, during, and after the American Revolution for artisans and businessmen of his time.

2. Paul Revere's Family History

Like many Americans both past and present, Paul Revere had ancestors who immigrated to America. Paul Revere's father, Apollos Rivoire, traveled from France to America and arrived early in 1716, at age thirteen.

Without a family in America, Apollos Rivoire was indentured to a Boston goldsmith, John Coney, who would pay for Rivoire's care in America in exchange for his work as an apprentice goldsmith. Although they were called goldsmiths, these men mainly worked in silver because gold was too expensive for most people to buy.

Like many people who came to America, Apollos Rivoire changed his name to a more English sounding, or Americanized, name. Apollos was shortened to Paul, and Rivoire evolved to Revere. A letter from young Paul Revere to his cousin dated around 1775 explains that his father changed his name to Paul Revere so "the Bumpkins should pronounce it easier."

By 1730, Paul Revere's father had finished his apprenticeship. He owned his own silver shop. In this

This bookplate by Paul Revere Sr. is thought to have been engraved in the 1720s. He may have changed his name, but he still considered himself a French gentleman. It is thought that he borrowed the design from the coat of arms of the De Rivoire family of eastern France, although there is probably no connection between the two families. This appears courtesy of the American Antiquarian Society.

year, the *Boston News-Letter* announced that he was moving his silversmith shop to the North End of Boston.

Around the time that he was able to start his own shop, Paul Revere Sr. married Deborah Hitchbourn. Although the Hitchbourns were not part of the very wealthy upper class, they were a well-established New England artisan family. Deborah's great-grandfather had arrived in America from England in 1641.

Deborah Hitchbourn and Paul Revere Sr. were married in the summer of 1729. With a new silversmith shop in the North End of Boston, the new Revere family began to expand. During their married life, Deborah and Paul Revere Sr. had twelve children but only seven survived past childhood. At this time, families had many children and many of these children died young.

3. Paul Revere's Childhood in Colonial Boston

Paul Revere was born in late December 1734. It is most likely that he was born at home, as most babies were in colonial times. His baptism is recorded at the New Brick Church in Boston on January 1, 1735. At this time, children were baptized shortly after they were born, so Paul Revere may have actually been born the day before he was baptized.

Paul Revere grew up in the North End of Boston. The Boston of Paul Revere's time was different from the Boston of today. The people were not as spread out as they are today. Everyone in Boston lived and worked by the wharves, or piers, in Boston Harbor. Paul Revere grew up surrounded by the sights and sounds of bustling activity in the crowded city. Wealthy merchants, enterprising shop owners and craftsmen, as well as poorer people all lived within the same areas of the city.

Colonial Boston was in some ways like a medieval European city with its winding narrow streets and close buildings. Street vendors sold oysters, fish, fruit, and vegetables from sacks on their backs or carts they

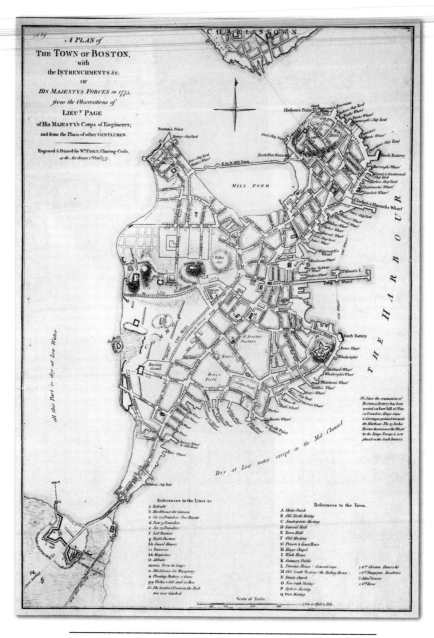

This 1777 plan of the town of Boston shows where the British were camped in 1775. It was based on the observations of a British soldier named Lieutenant Page and on the plans of other gentlemen. Boston's position on the coastline and its busy trade made it an attractive city for the British to occupy. Boston looked much like this while Paul Revere was growing up.

Left: This 1787 engraving by Treuchard is called "A View of the Town of Boston the Capital of New England." The tall spires in the engraving are churches. *Right:* In modern Boston, the churches have been replaced by skyscrapers.

The Boston of Paul Revere's time was very different from the Boston that stands today. The skyscrapers of the financial district now stand where colonial houses once were. The areas around the city, where Paul Revere rode on trails during his famous midnight ride, are no longer farmland. They are suburbs where millions of people live connected by highways and a subway known as the "T". Most remarkable in the growth of Boston is that much of present-day downtown Boston was underwater in Paul Revere's time! Today when visiting Boston, you will find that most of the streets that run in straight lines are newer streets. The curving streets and close buildings that remain in some areas of the North End are all that is left of the Boston in which Paul Revere lived.

pushed around the city. Domesticated animals such as pigs and chickens could be seen in the street.

In pre-Revolutionary Boston, the wharf was the center of activity in a city that thrived on a lively merchant trade. Wharves were not just places where ships were loaded and unloaded. The wharves and waterfront areas contained many shops and other places for people to buy and sell goods such as fish, rum, tar, and rope.

According to one source, there were fifteen churches in Boston in 1735. The inhabitants of Boston in Paul Revere's time were very religious and spent a lot of time in church. Churches provided a common place to meet and were used for political and social matters as well as for religious ones.

This is a bell made by Paul Revere. It is viewable at the Paul Revere House in Boston, Massachusetts.

There were also many church bells in the town of Boston that rang several times every day. Bells announced births and deaths, called people together, and signaled the opening and closing of markets. Around 1750, when Paul Revere was in his early teens, he and some of his friends were hired as bell ringers at Christ Church. Christ Church is known today as Old North Church, the same church in which the signal lanterns were hung on the night of Paul Revere's midnight ride in 1775.

To be a bell ringer, Paul Revere and his friends created and signed a special bell ringers' agreement. The document explained that the duty of the bell ringer was "Once a week on evenings to ring the bells for two hours." After signing the document, Paul Revere and his friends considered themselves to be part of a society of bell ringers. The last sentence of the agreement reads, "All Differences to be desided By a Majority of Voices." So everybody in the bell ringers' society had a vote. Paul Revere and his friends had experience with this small, democratic society at an early age. This may have influenced Paul Revere's thinking later in life.

Before Paul Revere signed the bell ringers' agreement, he was most likely attending school. School in colonial times was not like it is today. Girls did not go to school but were sometimes taught reading and writing at home. The few African children in Boston at the time would not have attended schools, either. Boys in Boston either went to a Latin school or a writing school.

Parents who could afford it sent their children to Latin schools. Latin schools prepared children for college and eventually for a profession, such as medicine or law. In Boston, children who graduated from Latin schools often went on to Harvard College. Writing schools were for children destined to become artisans or craftsmen. In these schools, children learned the basics of reading, writing,

We the Subscribers Do agree To the following Articles Viz

That if we Can have Liberty from the wardens of Doctor Cuttlers church we will Attend there once a week on Evenings To Ring the Bells for two hours Each Time from the date here of for one year

That we will Choose a Moderator Every three Month whose Business shall be To give out the Changes and other Business as shall be Agreed by a Majority of Voices then Present

That None shall Be admitted a Member of this Society without a Unanimous Vote of the Members then Present and that No member Shall begg Money of any Person for the Tower on Penalty of being Excluded the Society and that we will Attend To Ring at any Time when the Wardens of the Church Aforesaid shall desire it on Penalty of Paying three shillings for the good of the Society Provided we Can have the whole Care of the Bells

That the Members of this Society shall nott Exceed Eight Persons

and all Differences To be desided By a Majority of Voices

> John Pyer
> Paul Revere
> Josiah Flagg
> Barthw Bernard
> Jonathan Law
> Jona Brown junr
> Joseph Snelling

Society to Ring the Bells of Christ Church
Formed about 1750 by Paul Revere and his friends

This is a facsimile of the bell ringers' agreement signed by Paul Revere and his friends in about 1750. It was a democratic society in which each member had a voice in decision making. Paul Revere would continue to be an advocate of democracy for the rest of his life.

and math. Paul Revere probably attended the North Writing School on Love Lane in Boston.

Unlike schools today, the North Writing School taught reading in one room and writing in another. There were no grade levels and all students were probably taught the same lessons. The methods of teaching were also different from today. To force young boys to memorize lessons, teachers used harsh discipline, such as paddling or spanking.

4. Paul Revere's Life as a Young Adult

Paul Revere probably attended formal school for only four or five years. After that, like many boys his age, he would be ready to become an apprentice to learn a trade. Young men became apprentices as early as age thirteen. Paul Revere began his adult life as a silversmith apprentice under the instruction of his father.

These gold buttons were made by Paul Revere Sr. between 1725 and 1735. They show how skilled he was as an artisan, as round buttons were extremely difficult to make.

At first, Paul Revere would have performed small tasks while watching his father work. Over time, Paul Revere would have learned to do more and more in the shop. When he became good enough, he may have started making smaller items, like silver buttons and buckles for shoes and belts.

Paul Revere became a good silversmith quickly. In 1754, Paul Revere's father died. Paul Revere was only nineteen years old, so by law he could not inherit the silversmith business because he was not yet old enough. Even though Revere

Young Paul Revere would have watched his father make items like this tankard, made by Paul Revere Sr. between 1740 and 1754. The tankard is typical of New England tankards of the time. Though the body of the tankard is marked by Revere Sr., it recently has been discovered that the handle is marked with the initials "ws." It was thought that such sharing of parts did not happen until later in the eighteenth century, but this seems to prove otherwise.

could not own the shop, he and his younger brother, Thomas, carried on the family silversmith business. Most likely, Revere's mother became the formal owner of the business. She may have hired a journeyman to run the shop formally until Paul Revere was old enough to take over.

Still very much a young man, in early 1756, Paul Revere left the silversmith shop and went to fight in what became known as the French and Indian War. The British, French, and Native American allies on each

This undated engraving shows the defeat of General Braddock in the French and Indian War in 1755. Edward Braddock and his men were on their way to capture Fort Duquesne, but were surprised by French and Indian troops. Braddock was wounded and died a few days later. Both the British and the French were fighting over land rights and the rich resources in America. Despite what the name of the war implies, both sides had Indian allies.

side had been struggling for control of North America, and the rich resources and trade it provided, since 1645.

Men from Massachusetts were called on to fight with the British army to defend British interests and their own land. Many men from Boston and the countryside had been fighting these same wars for many years. The Massachusetts colonists were required to send groups of men, known as the militia, from each town to fight. Paul Revere was one of the many men who volunteered in Boston and who served as a lieutenant in an expedition to Crown Point in upstate New York. The mission was largely a failure because the troops did not capture the French fortress. Paul Revere never fought against the French troops, and he was returned to Boston in November 1756.

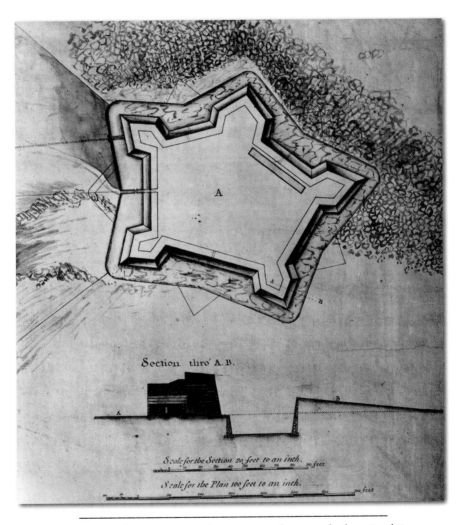

Section thro' A.B.

Scale for the Section 20 feet to an inch.

Scale for the Plan 100 feet to an inch.

This is a plan of Crown Point from 1755, the year before Paul Revere and other Massachusetts militiamen were sent to capture the French fort. The fort, located in upstate New York, would be the site of many battles in both the French and Indian War and the Revolutionary War.

5. Paul Revere's Family Life and Career as a Silversmith

Back in Boston, Revere returned to the silversmith shop where he was now master. For about the next fifty years, from 1756 to the early 1800s, Paul Revere would establish himself as one of the finest silversmiths in the colonies. During these fifty years, he also completed his famous midnight ride and, in the process, helped to win independence for America. Revere married twice and had a large family.

In 1757, the year after Revere returned to Boston, he married his first wife, Sarah Orne. About nine months later, they had their first child, Deborah, named for Paul Revere's mother. Not much is known about Sarah Orne. She was from a family of artisans from Salem and Boston, Massachusetts. Sarah had eight children with Paul Revere.

Right: Paul Revere's family tree shows the children he had in his two marriages, the first to Sarah Orne and the second to Rachel Walker. Note that several of the children from both marriages died at very young ages, as was very common during this time.

Paul Revere's Family

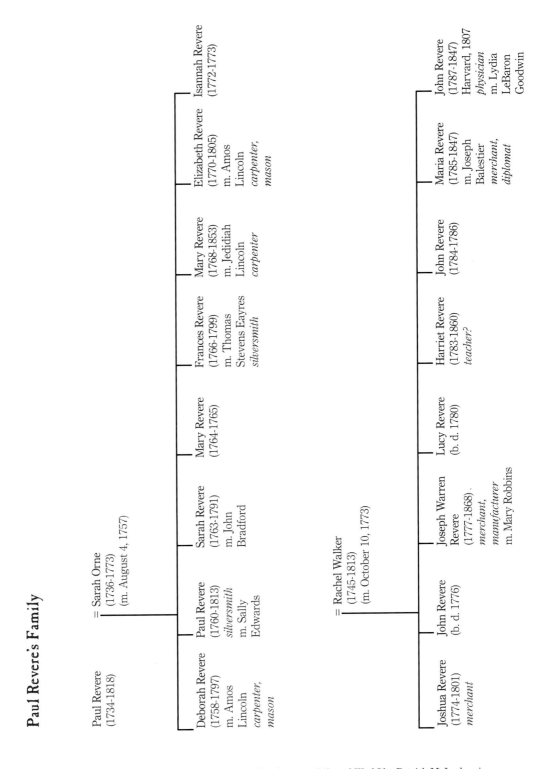

Paul Revere
(1734-1818)

= Sarah Orne
(1736-1773)
(m. August 4, 1757)

Deborah Revere
(1758-1797)
m. Amos
Lincoln
carpenter,
mason

Paul Revere
(1760-1813)
silversmith
m. Sally
Edwards

Sarah Revere
(1763-1791)
m. John
Bradford

Mary Revere
(1764-1765)

Frances Revere
(1766-1799)
m. Thomas
Stevens Eayres
silversmith

Mary Revere
(1768-1853)
m. Jedidiah
Lincoln
carpenter

Elizabeth Revere
(1770-1805)
m. Amos
Lincoln
carpenter,
mason

Isannah Revere
(1772-1773)

= Rachel Walker
(1745-1813)
(m. October 10, 1773)

Joshua Revere
(1774-1801)
merchant

John Revere
(b. d. 1776)

Joseph Warren
Revere
(1777-1868)
merchant,
manufacturer
m. Mary Robbins

Lucy Revere
(b. d. 1780)

Harriet Revere
(1783-1860)
teacher?

John Revere
(1784-1786)

Maria Revere
(1785-1847)
m. Joseph
Balestier
merchant,
diplomat

John Revere
(1787-1847)
Harvard, 1807
physician
m. Lydia
LeBaron
Goodwin

Source: "Reconstructing Paul Revere—An Overview of His Ancestry, Life and Work" by Patrick M. Leehey, in
Paul Revere—Artisan, Businessman, and Patriot: The Man Behind the Myth. (Paul Revere Association, 1988)

This 1771 engraving of a silvershop workbench is from an encyclo-pedia of the arts and sciences by Denis Diderot. The leather aprons, labeled with an *F* in the drawing, were used to collect scrap silver and filings. These filings were kept for use in other silver products.

Taking over the silversmith shop in 1756 allowed Paul Revere to provide for his large family. Paul Revere would have none of the problems experienced by other journeymen who wanted to set up shops. His father left him the shop, all of the tools, materials, and most impor-tant, clients. Most of the people who used to go to Paul Revere's father for new silver objects and silver repairs would come to Paul Revere.

The silver objects made in Revere's shop are worth a lot of money today. Many of the best pieces are in museums, like the Museum of Fine Arts in Boston. Silver from Revere's shop is a lot more valuable than similar works by other colonial silversmiths. This is true despite the fact that, although it is very good, Revere's silver is not always the best example of silver craftsmanship. Most scholars would agree that Revere's silver is so much more collectible because of his legendary midnight ride and his political life outside the silver shop.

Finished items made in Paul Revere's shop were stamped with his mark, PR. Other marks included P•Revere, Revere, and •Revere. These marks are used today to tell if a piece of silver was actually from Paul Revere's shop. In the beginning, Revere made much of the silver himself as he established himself as a master craftsman. However, not every piece of silver from his shop was made or repaired personally by Paul Revere. His apprentices, including his brother Thomas, and later his son Paul, would assist in making much of the silver that came out of Paul Revere's shop.

The business records before 1761 are probably lost. However, from 1761 onward we are able to keep track of Revere's business dealings in ledgers known as waste and memoranda books. These books cover the operation of Revere's shop in the years from 1761 to 1775, and from 1779 to 1797. By looking at the accounts of Revere's shop, we can learn

This is a section from Paul Revere's daybook, volume I, 1761–1783, from the Revere family papers. The entry in this waste and memoranda Book is dated January 8, 1763. Each entry lists who he has done work for and what he has made for them from a cream pot to six teaspoons to silver buckles for Joshua Brackett's shoes.

about what silver he made. We also can see how events outside the silver shop affected his business. The absence of records between 1775 and 1779, for example, reflect the period during the Revolutionary War when the silversmith shop was not really in operation.

From 1761 until 1764, business at Paul Revere's silver shop was very good. The French and Indian War brought a lot of money to Boston. Boston was a central port for ships coming and going with supplies and men. The merchants in Boston made profits from supplying the British army. As the merchants in Boston were making money, they were using some of it to buy silver from Paul Revere.

In 1764, one of Paul Revere's children came down with smallpox. This was an extremely dangerous and deadly disease. Colonial towns like Boston set aside buildings to house people with smallpox in the hopes of stopping the spread of the disease. These places sometimes were called hospitals, but more often they were called pesthouses. Despite the risk of infection, Revere did not send his child to a pesthouse, where the child probably would have died. Instead, the Revere family returned to their house and stayed there, under guard, until the smallpox was gone. None of Revere's family died from the disease.

This smallpox outbreak helps to explain why Revere's shop did not produce as much silver in 1764 as before. Times did not get better in 1765. Massachusetts entered into a postwar depression. The merchants of Boston were no longer making money off the war and supplying the British army. With fewer goods being shipped and merchants going bankrupt, they no longer needed new ships to be built or sails to be made. This put many sailmakers, shipbuilders, and sailors out of work. Any work that could be found did not pay as well and jobs were not easy to find.

As the people of Boston found themselves with less

THE Massachusetts Spy:
Or, Thomas's Boston Journal.

'Do thou Great LIBERTY inspire our Souls—And make our Lives in thy Possession happy—Or, our Deaths glorious in thy just Defence.'

(VOL. IV.)   THURSDAY, JULY 7, 1774.   (NUMB. 179.)

JOIN OR DIE

THE great demand for this paper, has often occasioned many good customers being disappointed, for which the publisher is very sorry: He will, in future, endeavour to prevent any thing of the like kind happening, so long as he may have the honour of being an humble-servant to the public.

The gloomy prospect of public affairs, at present, in this devoted capital, has occasioned some pressing Demands upon him, which with great reluctance he informs his customers, he can by no means answer without their kind assistance: He is loath to trouble them with a

In the House of Representatives, June 14, 1774.

WHEREAS there will become due in this month, sundry notes given by the province-treasurer, and sufficient provision having been made for the paying off the same, and if the possessors of such notes should not bring them in to the treasurer to be paid, the province will suffer damage by such neglect:

Therefore Resolved, That the possessors of such notes, who shall not bring them to the province-treasurer, to be paid by the last day of July next, shall not receive any interest on the same, after that time; and the province treasurer, is hereby directed forthwith to cause this order to be published in all the Boston News-papers, three weeks successively that every one concerned may be notified hereof.

Sent up for concurrence.
T. CUSHING, speaker

In council, June 15th,   Read and concurred.
JOHN COTTON, D. sec'ry.

Riots and weak publications, by a small number of individuals, are sufficient reasons with Parliament to ruin many thousand inhabitants of a truly respectable town, to dissolve charters, to abolish the benefits of the writ of *habeas corpus*, and extirpate American liberty—for the principle reaches all. But in *England* the press groans with publications, seditious, treasonable and even blasphemous. The discontented swarm over the kingdom, proclaiming their refinements. Many enormous riots have disturbed the public peace. The sovereign has been insulted in passing from his palace to the Parliament-house, on the business of the nation. Is it to be dreaded from these facts, that the BODY of THE PEOPLE is seditious and traiterous? can his Majesty believe, that he is thought by his English subjects in general, to be such a prince, as some of them have represented him? will the two houses of Parliament acknowledge what has been spoken and written and acted

adversus validissimas gentis pro nobis utilius, quam quod in Communi Noncosulunt. Rarus ad propusfandum commune periculum conventus. Ita dum singuli pugnant omnes vincuntur.‡

Why did the little Swiss cantons, and seven small provinces of the low countries, so successfully oppose the tyrants, that not contended with an empire founded in humanity and mutual advantages, *unmercifully* and arrogantly strove to "LAY" the faithful and affectionate wretches "AT THEIR FEET?" Because, they wisely regarded the interest of each as the interest of *all*.

Our own experience furnishes a mournful additional proof of an observation made by a great and good man, Lord president *Forbes*. "It is a certain truth," says he, "that all states and kingdoms, in proportion as they grow great, wealthy and powerful, grow wanton, wicked and oppressive, and the history of all ages gives evidence of the fatal catastrophe money, they first cut back on the expensive items, like the silver from Revere's shop. In times when his silversmith business was slow, Revere was resourceful and branched out into other businesses. He began to do work engraving copper, using the skills learned from engraving details onto his silver pieces. His engraving work included illustrations for magazines and broadsides.

Paul Revere also took up dentistry and became known for creating and fitting false teeth. Newspapers of the day contained advertisements for his new abilities as a dentist who sold and fitted false teeth. He was not a trained dentist, but Paul Revere sold false teeth, cleaned them, and wired them into his clients' mouths. There was even a legend that Paul Revere made George Washington's false teeth, but these claims were untrue.

Left: Paul Revere engraved the masthead of the July 7, 1774, issue of the *Massachusetts Spy Or Thomas's Boston Journal,* Vol IV. Notice that the snake is broken into segments representing the colonies and that it faces the royal lion. The words "Join or Die" are above the snake, meaning that the only way they can strike against the crown is to be united.

6. Paul Revere's Early Political Life

The declining prosperity after the French and Indian War was not only felt in Boston. The government in England was feeling it, too. In 1761, to make back some of the money spent on the war, Britain attempted to collect taxes from the colonies. The colonists had always been taxed on many of the goods that came in and out of the busy port of Boston. In the past, however, the merchants often had not paid these taxes. In fact, many wealthy merchants, like John Hancock, made their fortunes smuggling goods to avoid paying taxes.

The British parliament had not enforced the laws in the past because Britain still profited from the trade between itself and the colonies. The French and Indian War cost Britain a lot of money. After the war, Britain was looking for a way to make more money especially to pay off war debts. The British army fought side by side with militiamen like Revere during the war. For this protection of the colonies, Parliament decided to enforce the taxes already in place.

In 1760, customs officials, or tax collectors, began to enforce the Navigation Acts, which Boston merchants

This is a portrait of John Hancock by John Singleton Copley.

John Hancock was born on January 23, 1737, in Braintree (now Quincy), Massachusetts. He was raised by his uncle, Thomas Hancock, a wealthy Boston merchant, who adopted him on his father's death. After graduating from Harvard in 1754, Hancock joined his uncle's firm, and ten years later he took over, becoming the wealthiest merchant in New England. He joined the protest against the Stamp Act, as he stood to suffer a great deal from the British taxation of his business. He was elected the president of the Continental Congress and made his famous signature on the Declaration of Independence. After the Revolution, Hancock was elected as governor of Massachusetts. He died on October 8, 1793.

had avoided for years. The merchants in Boston argued that the newly enforced taxes were unfair and would slow down the prosperous businesses they had. The merchants could not argue that they should be allowed to smuggle goods without paying taxes. So instead of focusing on the taxes, the colonists said the merchants, as Englishmen, had a natural freedom from the illegal searches of property and seizure of goods used to collect taxes.

Outside the courts, people gathered to discuss the enforcement of taxes in the many social and professional societies. One of these societies was the Masons, which Paul Revere joined in 1760. Revere would remain an active Mason for the rest of his life. Masonic societies were limited to professional men who were doctors, lawyers, merchants, and artisans like Revere. It was important for Paul Revere's business that he became a Mason. Many of his best clients or possible clients would be Masons. Eventually Revere's silver shop was asked to make the medals and badges that the Masons of his lodge and other related lodges wore.

Without organizations like the Masons, an artisan such as Paul Revere would not have contact with lawyers or doctors except on a professional basis. The Masons brought some of the different levels of Boston society together into one organization. They were secretive in their rituals but were very powerful because of the status of the members involved. These were men prepared to act as they discussed the taxes being enforced and the

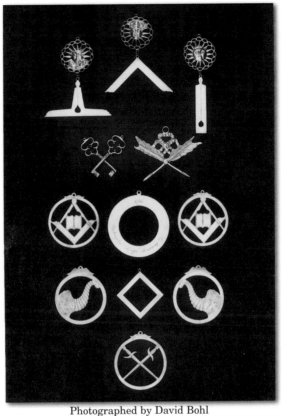

Photographed by David Bohl

In addition to medals, Paul Revere crafted Masonic jewels to be worn by lodge officers. This set of twelve silver Masonic jewels was made by Revere in 1796 for the Washington Lodge. When Revere was Grand Master, he helped found this particular lodge. Each jewel signifies an office within the lodge. For instance, in the second row from the top, the keys belonged to the treasurer, and the quill pens to the secretary.

role of the British government in Boston.

As people struggled to find work and faced bank-ruptcy, they started looking for someone to blame. The colonists focused their frustration and anger on Parliament and the enforcement of taxes on the colonies. The people of Massachusetts felt that they should not be made to pay for the British army. The

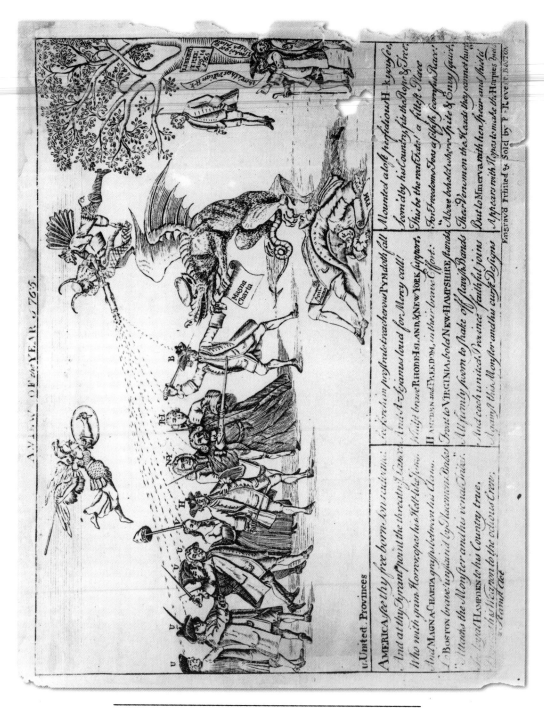

This is the 1765 engraving by Paul Revere called *A View of the Year 1765*. Each person in the group on the left represents one of the colonies as they unite to fight against the king and his tyrannical rule, represented by the serpent with the Magna Carta grasped in its claws. Notice the tax collector hanging in the Liberty Tree.

French had been defeated and there was no longer a serious threat of invasion from the North. The colonists felt the enforcement of tax collection was at the expense of their rights as Englishmen. Most of all, the colonists had never been taxed heavily before, and they did not want to be taxed heavily now.

In 1765, Paul Revere actually went into debt but was able to settle out of court. In the same year, he became a founding member of the Sons of Liberty. The Sons of Liberty was similar to a Masonic society with secret symbols and passwords. They often met in the taverns and inns around the city, like the Green Dragon

This 1773 ink and watercolor drawing by John Johnson shows the Green Dragon Tavern, in operation since 1712. The tavern was a large brick building that had been modeled on the Green Dragon Tavern in Bishopsgate, London. It became a center for Revolutionary activity and was purchased by Revere's Masonic lodge. This is shown by the square and compass in the upper left corner.

Tavern. The Sons of Liberty came together to discuss, protest, and organize against what they felt was unfair taxation and treatment by Britain.

Colonists that were against the enforcement of taxation and the resulting unfair treatment by Britain were known as Whigs. Today we call these people patriots, or revolutionaries. In 1765, there were still many people in Boston who were against excessive taxation by the British, but they felt themselves to be citizens of the British Empire.

As tensions increased, almost every person and family in Boston and throughout the colonies chose a side. The people in the colonies who continued to agree with the British were known as loyalists, or Tories. These loyalists did not agree with the Whigs and they did not want an extreme change. Often loyalists were important people who worked for the British as tax collectors or in other positions. Loyalists were often attacked or scared by the mobs of Whig supporters in the towns.

Despite the rising tensions, Britain decided to collect a new tax from the colonies. The enforcement of old tax laws in the American colonies did not produce the money the British had expected. This was mainly because of the unwillingness of the colonists to pay. Britain still needed money to pay for the war, so Parliament passed the Stamp Act. The Stamp Act required that stamps be purchased and attached to all printed materials, such as business documents and newspapers. The colonists, not just in Massachusetts,

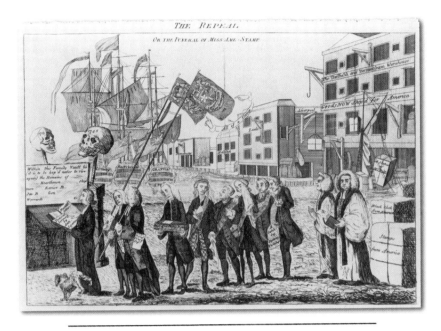

This cartoon was published in a London paper on the day the king repealed the Stamp Act. The cartoon made fun of First Lord of the Treasury George Grenville, here called George Stamper, and his supporters for this and other unpopular taxes. Grenville carries a small coffin holding his child, the Stamp Act. The two banners being carried by his supporters represent the parliamentary votes, spearheaded by William Pitt, against the act.

but in most of the colonies, would not accept such an unfair tax from Britain. In Boston, the Sons of Liberty led the often-violent protests against the Stamp Act.

There were so many protests about the Stamp Act that it never was enforced. Protests were common in the years before the Revolution as various actions by the British continued to anger the colonists. Paul Revere probably played a key role in organizing and taking part in many of these protests.

This is a portrait of Samuel Adams by John Singleton Copley.

Samuel Adams was a Harvard graduate from the powerful and well-established Adams family. His cousin John Adams and nephew John Quincy Adams went on to serve as presidents of the United States. Samuel Adams had tried several businesses, including a brewery, but was not very successful. He was a better revolutionary. He knew how to use events like the Boston Massacre and the Boston Tea Party to his advantage. Samuel Adams was one of the creators of the Committees of Correspondence. He also signed the Declaration of Independence.

In the coming years, Paul Revere would join many of the most influential clubs supporting the Whig cause. He joined the North Caucus, which was smaller than the Sons of Liberty but more political. Revere also was invited to join the Long Room Club, a small circle of about seventeen members that included most of the leaders in pre-Revolutionary Boston, including Samuel Adams, John Hancock, Joseph Warren, James Otis, and Benjamin Church. Most of the leaders were Harvard-educated doctors, lawyers, merchants, and other businessmen. Paul Revere was an artisan with links to the business, or working, class of people like himself. As such, his was an important voice in the Long Room Club.

The colonists' victory over the Stamp Act did not last very long. The British still needed money to finance the government. In 1767, shortly after the defeat of the Stamp Act, the British passed the Townshend Acts. The Townshend Acts put a duty on a few goods, such as tea, glass, and paper, in hopes of raising some more money for the government in London.

The colony of Massachusetts sent out a Circular Letter to the rest of the colonies urging them not to pay taxes on the goods in the Townshend Acts. King George III and the government in Britain were so upset by this Circular Letter that they ordered Massachusetts to rescind it, or to take it back. The Massachusetts legislature voted not to rescind the letter by a vote of

This is a 1765 portrait of Joseph Warren by Edward Savage, after the original by John Singleton Copley. Warren graduated from Harvard in 1759 and went on to study medicine. He became one of the most well-respected doctors in the colonies. He was the man who ordered Paul Revere to Lexington and Concord to warn of the British arrival. He was killed during the Battle of Bunker Hill, in June 1775.

ninety-two to seventeen. To remember this event, Paul Revere made one of his most important works, *The Sons of Liberty or Rescinders' Bowl*. The bowl was made to honor the "Glorious 92" who voted not to rescind the Circular Letter. It is decorated with symbols of liberty.

This bowl went on to become a symbol of freedom and of the American Revolution. Paul Revere, with his skills as an engraver and silversmith, would help to document the events and rising tensions that led to his midnight ride and to the Revolutionary War. Revere also made several political cartoon engravings and an often-used engraving of the British ships entering

Paul Revere made the Rescinders' Bowl for the 92 members of the Massachusetts House of Representatives who voted not to give in to the "insolent Menaces of the Villains in Power," and would not rescind the Circular Letter written in protest of the Townshend Acts. The names of the people who ordered it from Revere are inscribed around the rim, and there are various symbols of liberty engraved on the bowl.

Boston. His most well-known engraving is of the Boston Massacre. From these works, we can see how active and important Paul Revere was in the Revolutionary movement.

To punish the colonists for not following the orders of the British king, on September 30, 1768, the British army was sent into Boston as a show of force. The British army and navy made a big show as they sailed into Boston and marched ashore. Paul Revere must have observed this entrance, as he went back to his silversmith shop and created an engraving to commemorate the event. He called it *The Insolent Parade*.

The British general Thomas Gage was in charge of the army in North America. He was sent to Boston to oversee the army's movements in the city. The British wanted to show their power in dealing with rebellious colonists. General Gage ordered his army to be disciplined when interacting with the citizens of Boston, but this was often hard for the soldiers who were taunted and teased as "redcoats" or "lobsterbacks."

The closeness of the British army to the citizens of Boston was causing a lot of tension. On the night of March 5, 1770, in the cold streets of Boston, the tensions came to a head. British soldiers fired on a crowd of Boston citizens who were throwing ice at them and calling them names. Five Boston citizens in the crowd died and several others were wounded. A large number of British troops were able to get to the scene and

GENERAL the HON'ble THO.ˢ GAGE
OB.ᵗ 1788

General Thomas Gage fought with the British army against the French and Scottish before fighting in the French and Indian War in 1756. After this war, General Gage was put in charge of the whole British army in North America. He was the most powerful British official in the colonies at the time of the Battle of Lexington and Concord. The above portrait was done in 1788.

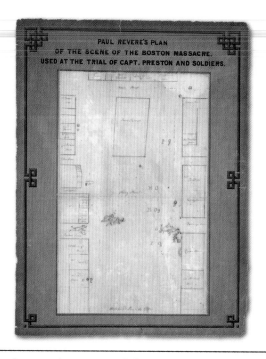

PAUL REVERE'S PLAN
OF THE SCENE OF THE BOSTON MASSACRE,
USED AT THE TRIAL OF CAPT. PRESTON AND SOLDIERS.

Paul Revere made two diagrams of the Boston Massacre. This diagram, which is in pen and ink on paper, shows the positions of the soldiers and citizens during the massacre. It was probably intended for use during the trials that followed the event. This was a more accurate depiction of the soldiers and citizens than the engraving on the opposite page.

prevent further bloodshed on that cold night. The event came to be known as the Boston Massacre.

Paul Revere's print of the Boston Massacre captured the political feelings of the time more than the accuracy of the event. The engraving shows the British exercising their power over the defenseless citizens. In fact, a British officer ordered his men not to fire. He tried to step between the soldiers and the crowd. Also, the massacre looks like it happened in bright daytime under a blue sky, but the real event took place on a dark, snowy,

This engraving was created by Paul Revere in March 1770. The original drawing was done by Henry Pelham, who was quite angry that Revere managed to print his version first. The picture served as a powerful propaganda piece, making the British soldiers appear organized and calculating. In reality they were in chaos as the unruly mob threatened them. Revere also added a sign reading Butcher's Hall above the Customs House to incite the colonists' anger further.

winter night. Paul Revere also added a sign reading Butcher's Hall over a house behind the British soldiers.

The town of Boston was outraged by this event. Every year, starting from 1770, the Sons of Liberty organized a large demonstration on the anniversary of the massacre. The revolutionary leaders in Boston used the massacre and other tragic events, such as the murder of Christopher Snyder by a British soldier, to their advantage. The March 11, 1771, issue of the *Boston Gazette* reported that "In the evening, there was a very striking Exhibition at the Dwelling House of Mr. Paul Revere, fronting old North Square. At one of the Chamber

The Paul Revere House, built in 1680 in the North End, stands as the oldest building in downtown Boston. Revere lived in the house for many years. One can visit the house today and see many artifacts related to Revere and his life.

Windows was the Appearance of the Ghost of the unfortunate Snyder."

In 1770, Revere and his growing family purchased the house in old North Square mentioned in the newspaper article. The house still stands today in Boston's North End, and is now home to the Paul Revere Memorial Association. Although Revere moved later in life, the house in old North Square was the one Paul Revere lived in just before and during the Revolution.

Sarah Revere only lived in the new house for three years. She died in 1773 after giving birth to their eighth child. This child of Paul and Sarah Revere also died young. The demands of eight childbirths were too much for Sarah Revere's body, just as they were for many women of her time.

It was more than five months after Sarah's death when Paul Revere married his second wife, Rachel Walker. She was from a good family, and she seemed very active, lively, and able to take on a family with six surviving children. Paul and Rachel Revere would also have eight children together through the years, although three would die young.

7. Paul Revere and the Coming Revolution

All the activity in Paul Revere's life at home was occurring as the colonies were protesting over tea from Britain. The very day of the Boston Massacre, the British parliament repealed the hated Townshend Acts but left a small tax on tea. For about two years, things were relatively quiet. The event that triggered more rebellious acts in Boston and the colonies was the Tea Act of 1773. The act, which taxed tea in both England and the colonies, was meant to help the British East India Company raise money to cover debts from poor sales, the company's overpurchase of tea, and the need to build forts in India to defend against possible French attack.

To the colonists, the Tea Act seemed like another example of the British imposing their power over the colonies. The price of tea was set artificially low, and only certain selected merchants were allowed to sell the cheap tea. The rest of the merchants in Boston were not able to sell the tea from the British East India Company, which threatened to put them out of business. The anger toward the new Tea Act was not limited just to Boston.

Many colonies resisted it. The British government ordered the tea to be sent to Boston, anyway.

The Sons of Liberty organized a resistance to the tea that was being shipped to Boston. It would result in the incident now known as the Boston Tea Party. The Sons of Liberty dressed up as Native Americans, using black soot from lamps to darken their skin and hide their true identities.

On December 16, 1773, many people in Boston turned out to watch the Sons of Liberty open boxes of tea with their axes and dump tons of tea into Boston Harbor. The harbor was said to be brown with tea when they were done. The Sons of Liberty were highly organized. They made a point not to steal the other property on the ships and not to hurt anyone. They wanted to stay within what they felt was the law, and within their right to protest.

They also wanted to make sure their version of the Boston Tea Party reached the other colonies before the British version did. To do this, Paul Revere recalled, "I was employed by the Select men of the Town of Boston to carry the Account of the Destruction of the Tea to New York." With little sleep after the long night before, Paul Revere rode for New York on December 17, 1773.

From the end of 1773 until the beginning of the Revolution in 1775, Paul Revere often was chosen to deliver important messages exchanged by the colonial leaders in distant cities. When the colonies received

This 1856 color engraving, by John Andrew, shows the Boston Tea Party of December 16, 1773. The men in the boat were patriots dressed as Mohawk Indians. In protest against a tax on tea, they threw the contents of 342 chests of tea into Boston Harbor. The British punished the colonists with the Coercive, or Intolerable, Acts.

news of the Boston Tea Party, most of them supported the actions of the Massachusetts colonists.

The Boston Tea Party outraged the British, and Parliament soon passed the Coercive Acts. These acts were known as the Intolerable Acts to the colonists. They were "intolerable" because they closed the port of Boston, canceled the Massachusetts colonial charter, and restricted town meetings. The port of Boston was supposed to be closed down until the colonists agreed to pay for all the tea they had destroyed. The colonists refused to pay for the tea, even though they had always

As rebels against British government orders, the men who participated in the Boston Tea Party risked arrest and the loss of their businesses. The Native American disguises did not mean that the people of Boston did not know the main actors in the Boston Tea Party. Shortly after the event, the people in Boston could be heard singing this part of the following song:

Rally Mohawks! Bring out your axes,
And tell King George we'll pay no taxes
On his foreign tea. . .
Our Warren's there, and bold Revere
With hands to do and words to cheer
For Liberty and laws.

Although there is no proof that Joseph Warren and Paul Revere actually took part in the Boston Tea Party, this song indicates that they had some role in the event.

depended on the operation of Boston's wharves and port for jobs, money, goods, and food.

When news of the Intolerable Acts reached the colonies, Paul Revere rode between Philadelphia and Boston several times to help form the resistance. The Whig leaders in Boston developed the Suffolk Resolves in response to the Intolerable Acts. The Suffolk Resolves declared the actions of the British unlawful and urged resistance against them. The Resolves also advised towns in Massachusetts to organize their own governments, with militias to fight, if necessary.

It was Paul Revere who again rode from the Committee of Correspondence in Boston to the Continental Congress in Philadelphia to deliver the Suffolk Resolves. Part of the Suffolk Resolves was the recommendation that towns create companies of minutemen from their militias to defend against the British army. The minutemen were instructed to "Equip and hold themselves in readiness, on the shortest notice from the said committee of safety, to march to the place of rendezvous." Some New England towns created groups of minutemen in 1774, but many others had militias and special groups of minutemen that were already in existence and able to be ready in a short period of time.

The Continental Congress supported the actions of the Massachusetts colony when they heard the news. News brought by Revere and other express riders kept the people informed about what was happening in each colony. The British did not really expect the colonies, which were all very different and far apart, to be able to work together and support each other.

Because of this belief, General Thomas Gage focused on enforcing the Coercive Acts in Massachusetts and ignored the other colonies. General Gage planned to find out where the Massachusetts colonists were hiding their military supplies and to take them away. The hard part for General Gage was to conduct these missions quickly and quietly, so colonists would not be able to hide the supplies or prepare any resistance.

On September 1, 1774, about two hundred-sixty British soldiers were able to remove the largest supply of gunpowder in Massachusetts without any resistance. When the colonists found out that the gunpowder had been taken, an alarm went through the countryside.

The spread of the alarm was not very organized and there were many rumors of British attacks on Boston, but the colonists still managed to alert one another about the situation. This event became known as the Powder Alarm. General Gage had misjudged the the colonists' ability to organize and quickly come together.

After the Powder Alarm, the colonists did not want to be caught off guard again. In Boston, Paul Revere recalled that he "was one of upwards of thirty, chiefly mechanics, who formed ourselves into a committee for the purpose of watching the movements of the British

THE UNITED COLONIES

AT THE

BEGINNING OF THE REVOLUTION.

> *Spies played an important role in events leading up to the Battle of Lexington and Concord. The loyalist spy William Bratton informed General Gage that the colonists had been taking powder from the provincial powder house. This inspired General Gage to act fast and capture the rest of the powder.*

soldiers, and gaining every intelligence of the movements of the Tories." In other words, they were spies.

One of the most famous spies was Dr. Benjamin Church, who was a friend of Paul Revere and Dr. Joseph Warren. Dr. Church was involved in the most important and secret revolutionary clubs in Boston. He was also being bribed by General Gage to be a spy. Paul Revere recalled "That our meetings were discovered, and [this informant] mentioned the identical words that were spoken among us

---

Left: This map shows the colonies at the beginning of the Revolution. In a time without cars, trains, or planes, the colonies were far apart from each other and news traveled slowly. The colonists worked hard to communicate with each other during the Revolution because they knew the only way to defeat Britain was to work together.

the night before." None of the Whig leaders could figure out that it was Dr. Church who was telling every-thing to General Gage until after the Revolutionary War had begun.

According to Revere, he and others "frequently took Turns, two and two, to Watch the soldiers, By patrolling the Streets all night." This spying paid off in December 1774, when the colonists found out that the British planned to march to Fort William and Mary in New Hampshire. General Gage wanted the stores of gun-powder, small guns, and cannons from the old fort that was poorly guarded by a few British soldiers. He knew that if the stores remained in the fort, they would be at risk from the colonists.

Again, it was Paul Revere who was chosen to make the winter ride, this time up to Maine. On December 13, 1774, Revere warned the Portsmouth Committee of Correspondence of the possible British mission. Before the British could arrive from Boston, the Portsmouth militia was able to muster about 400 men and attack Fort William and Mary.

The few British soldiers guarding the fort were forced to surrender. The militiamen took the military supplies and hid them in neighboring towns. This event became known as the Portsmouth Alarm. The British were aware that it was Revere who was responsible for sounding the alarm. Lord Percy, who would later play an important role in the Battle of Lexington and

This engraving shows the British surrender of Fort William and Mary.
This attack and seizure of the fort by American colonists once again
proved the effectiveness of their advance alarm system. If information was gathered about British plans or troop movements, colonists
like Paul Revere were sent to warn the surrounding towns.

515. Lord Percy under attainder. Exh. 1831. TURNER Collection.

Lord Hugh Earl Percy served under British General Gage during the Revolutionary War. He came to America thinking the best of the colonists, but after just a few weeks in Boston, he wrote that they were "a set of sly, artful, hypocritical rascals, cruel, and cowards."

Concord, remembered that "Mr. Paul Revere (a person who is employed by the Committee of Correspondence, here, as a messenger) arrived at Portsmouth with a letter from the committee here to those of that place."

General Gage planned another secret attack on the military supplies in the town of Salem in early 1775. Revere and his secret committee of spies heard that the British were planning another expedition but needed more details. When Paul Revere and two others sailed to Castle Island in Boston Harbor to find out what they could, British soldiers captured them. Paul Revere and his two friends were held in prison from Saturday until Monday, after the mission was done. The mission to Salem was a failure for the British, and the troops were forced to go back to Boston empty-handed and discouraged.

The spirits of the British army were low. Food and water were becoming harder to find for both the British troops and the residents still in Boston. The British government wanted General Gage to make the people of Massachusetts pay for the tea they had destroyed.

At the beginning of 1775, about seven hundred more soldiers were sent to General Gage. A letter from London explained to Gage that the colonists were threatening the King's honor and the safety of the Empire. This "force should be repelled by force," the letter said. The British government also suggested that Gage "arrest and imprison the principal actors . . . of the Provincial Congress whose proceedings appear in every light to be acts of treason and rebellion." It is with the extra men that General Gage planned to raid the military supplies he knew were held in Concord.

When word of the order to capture leaders in the Provincial Congress reached the colonists, many of the most influential leaders packed up and left Boston. John Hancock and Samuel Adams were two important leaders who left town. Dr. Joseph Warren and Paul Revere decided to stay in Boston to keep an eye on any British developments.

8. Paul Revere's Midnight Ride

The Whigs who remained in Boston watched the British army for signs of more raids into the country-side. On April 7, 1775, the colonists noticed boats being brought from navy ships in Boston Harbor into the Back Bay. The Whig leaders also learned that some British soldiers were scouting out the roads to Concord. Led by Joseph Warren, the colonists decided to send Paul Revere to warn Concord of this new information.

On April 8, 1775, Revere rode to Concord with a letter from Joseph Warren that advised the town leaders that a force from the British army would be coming to remove all military supplies from the town. A loyalist in Concord reported to General Gage, "Last Saturday the 7th of April P:_ R:_ toward evening arrived at Concord." The loyalist used the wrong date (it was the eighth of April), but the rest of the message was correct.

At this time, the colonists did not know when the British would be coming, how large the force would be, or which route they would take to get from Boston. However, the information was enough to get the townspeople moving the ammunition and supplies into houses, into the woods, and to neighboring towns.

On April 15, 1775, General Gage moved some of his best soldiers to be ready for the mission to Concord. The movement of these troops was hard to hide from the Boston colonists. Two days before his midnight ride, Paul Revere made a trip to Lexington to warn John Hancock and Samuel Adams of the troop activity in Boston because it was assumed that the British might try to capture the leaders of the Massachusetts revolutionary movement.

On his way back into Boston, Revere stopped to meet with the town and militia leaders of the Charlestown Committee of Safety. There was a risk that the British would guard Boston so heavily that nobody would be allowed out to warn the countryside. Revere and the Committee of Safety developed an early warning system in case riders were not able to get out of Boston. Revere later recalled that "I agreed with a Col. Conant, and some other Gentleman, that if the British went out by Water, we would shew two lanthorns [lanterns] in the North Church Steeple; and if by Land, one, as a Signal."

News of Paul Revere's second trip also was reported to General Gage. A spy reported that many of the military supplies had already been moved out of Concord.

The British commander realized it would be difficult to get troops ready for a raid with Revere or other colonists warning the countryside about it. General Gage sent out groups of four or five soldiers with horses on the roads between Lexington, Concord, and Boston to try to stop any riders from raising the alarm.

On April 18, 1775, the British troops that were to march to Concord assembled on the Boston Common. According to Paul Revere's account of the night's events, Dr. Joseph Warren sent for him at about 10:00 P.M. Revere recalled that Warren wanted him "to go to Lexington and inform Mr. Samuel Adams, and the Hon. John Hancock Esqr. that there was a number of Soldiers . . . marching to the bottom of the common, where was a number Boats to receive them, and it was supposed, that they were going to Lexington, by the way of Watertown, and take them, Mess. Adams and Hancock, or to Concord."

Warren had already sent William Dawes to ride to Concord by land. William Dawes, like Revere, was an artisan from Boston. He too was involved in the Revolutionary activities, but not to the same extent as Revere. Like many patriots who helped warn the minutemen, William Dawes played a large role but is often forgotten when we talk about the alarm that was sounded that night. He risked capture by sneaking past the British guards at the narrow land entrance to Boston.

Shortly after Dawes left Boston, Paul Revere took a different path to Lexington by going across the Charles

This portrait of Major William Dawes is by Daniel Strain. Dawes was one of the many express riders during the time. He was asked to ride on April 18, 1775, because his business as a cordwainer, or shoe-maker and leatherworker, often took him through the British lines around Boston and he knew many of the guards. It was thought that he could slip through the area easily without being questioned.

River, to Charlestown. According to a later retelling of the events of that night, Paul Revere said that he "left Dr. Warren, called upon a friend and desired him to make the Signals." There may have been as many as three people who helped to light the signal lanterns in the steeple of the Old North Church, known as Christ Church in Paul Revere's time.

The lanterns were only lit for a few seconds but were seen by the waiting Committee of Safety members in Charlestown. It is not known if they were able to send out an express rider to warn the countryside that the British army was marching to Concord. Some claim that an express rider did leave from Charlestown but probably was captured by the British patrols that had been stationed along the roads to Concord and Lexington.

This is a replica of the signal lantern from Old North Church.

According to Paul Revere, after he told his friend to make the signals, he "went Home, took my Boots and Surtout, and went to the North part of Town, Where I had kept a Boat; two friends rowed me across Charles River, a little to the eastward where the Somerset Man of War lay." The *Somerset* was a large British navy ship, with sixty-four guns, known as a man-of-war, stationed in the Charles River to prevent anyone from crossing where

There are two folktales that surround the crossing of the river that may or may not be true. The first story is that Paul Revere was in such a hurry that he forgot the spurs needed for riding a horse. The story states that he sent his dog, which had followed him, from the docks back to the house with a note pinned to its collar. A short while later, the dog returned with Paul Revere's spurs in its mouth.

The second story is that Paul Revere's friends forgot coverings for the oars. Pieces of cloth were needed to silence the noise made when the oar handle rubbed oarlocks on the boat. Revere's friends snuck to a nearby friend's house, knocked on the window, and told her what they needed. She looked around her room and threw down some wool undergarments that, it was said, she may have been wearing. The two men were able to wrap the oars in these and row across the river in silence.

It is not known for sure if either of these stories is true, but they have been built into the telling and retelling of the story.

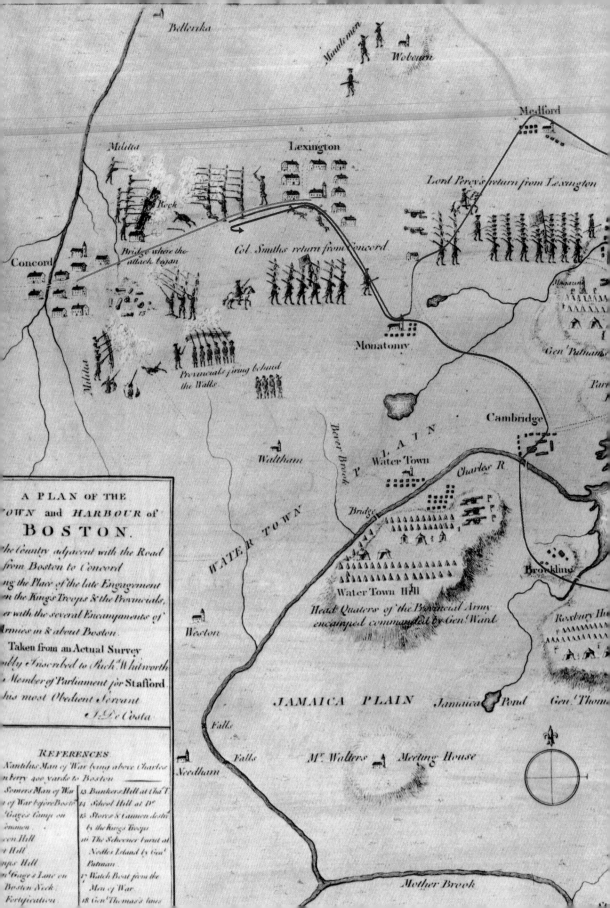

Salem

Marblehead

H...

Minutemen

Lynn

Malden

Bridges River

Nahant Rock

Chelsea

Winnisimit

Nahant Bay

Nahant Point

Hogg I.

...ampright to the Bridge perpetually of 62 acres

Penny Ferry

Medford R.

Hull

Noddles I.

...ps Farm

Charles Town

Ferry Boat

Winter

BROAD

BOSTON

Governors I.

Nix I.

Pudding Point

SOUND

Castle I.

Dorchester Neck

Deer I.

North Bruste...

Dorchester

Nix's Mate

Apthorpe

King Road

Gallops I.

Level I.

Little Bruste...

Thompsons I.

Spectacle I.

Georges I.

Great Bruster

Camp

Long I.

Been I.

Nantasket Road

Milton H.

Sheen I.

Rainforths I.

The prick'd line is the Ships Cha...

Hull

Point Alderto...

Milton

Hangman I.

Hogg I.

Pittick's I.

Moon I.

Bluehills

Quinsey Creek

Sheen I.

Pankins I.

the ferry usually crossed, between the cities of Boston and Charlestown.

The three men were able to cross the Charles undetected with help from an incoming tide and a bright moon, which hid them in the shadows. On the other side, Revere remembered, "When I got into Town, I met Col. Conant, and several others; they said they had seen our signals. I told them what was Acting, and went to git me a Horse; I got a Horse of Deacon Larkin."

The horse that Paul Revere rode during the midnight ride was not his own. Deacon Larkin of Charlestown provided it for him, and Paul Revere recalled it to have been "a very good horse." Through the years, many names have been made up for Paul Revere's horse, but tradition in the Larkin family has it that the actual name of the horse may have been Brown Beauty.

While Paul Revere was getting the horse ready, he learned of the British army officers that General Gage had sent ahead of time to prevent riders like Revere from sounding the alarm in Concord. Just after leaving Charlestown, Revere "saw two Officers on Horse-back, standing under the shade of a Tree, in a narrow part of the roade." In his account just after the ride, he recalled, "One of them Started his horse towards me,

Previous Spread: This map shows the routes that Paul Revere (highlighted in red), William Dawes (in blue) and Samuel Prescott (in orange) took to spread the alarm to Lexington and Concord that the British army was marching from Boston.

and the other up the road, as I supposed, to head me should I escape the first." Revere was able to escape by turning around and galloping to another road that would still take him to Lexington. Revere recalled that the British patrol "followed me about 300 Yardes, and finding He could not catch me, returned."

Paul Revere did not run into any more British patrols on his way to Lexington. After he escaped the first patrol, Paul Revere said, "In Medford, I awaked the Captain of the Minutemen; and after that, I alarmed almost every House, till I got to Lexington." Revere gave the initial alarm to the countryside, but

This 1931 oil painting by Grant Wood depicts the midnight ride of Paul Revere. The style of the painting is romantic, similar to the legends and poems that have been passed down. The tall church next to Revere and his horse indicate the righteousness of their cause. The solitary figure riding through an eerily still landscape also shows that Wood may be saying that such a ride lives more in the land of dreams than in reality.

The myths about Paul Revere's ride state that he rode through the towns yelling, "The British are coming!" This is not likely, because the colonists in Massachusetts were still British themselves. It is more likely that the British army would be called the Regulars, as William Munroe recalled Paul Revere saying.

there were many others after him who continued to spread the word to neighboring towns that the British regulars were marching. This alarm was essential in getting the minutemen who lived in these towns ready to go to Lexington and Concord.

In Lexington, Paul Revere "alarmed Mr. Adams and Col. Hancock." John Hancock and Samuel Adams were staying in Lexington at the house of the Reverend Jonas Clarke. There was a guard at the door of the Clarke house on the night of April 18 because Hancock and Samuel Adams were such important Revolutionary leaders. William Munroe, the guard and a town leader in Lexington recalled that when Revere arrived, "I told him, the family had just retired, and had requested, that they might not be disturbed by any noise about the house. 'Noise!' said he, 'you'll have noise enough before long. The regulars are coming out.'"

William Dawes finally arrived in Lexington shortly after Revere, and the two express riders headed off to Concord a short time later. As they rode toward Concord, Revere recalled, "We were overtaken by a young Doctor Prescot, whom we found to be a high Son of Liberty." Samuel Prescott, a young physician from Concord, told Paul Revere that he was willing to help spread the alarm.

On the way to Concord, Paul Revere proposed to the other two men "that we had better allarm all the Inhabitents till we got to Concord." This is what Revere had done on the first part of his ride from Boston. That is why the alarm system was so effective in getting the minutemen ready in time to meet the British.

Revere, Dawes, and Prescott were waking up the people in the houses along the road when they were captured by the British officers halfway between Lexington and Concord. Paul Revere wrote after the start of the war that "The other two, stopped at a House to awake the man, I kept along, when, I had got about 200 Yards a head of them, I saw two officers under as before." There were only two British soldiers, so Revere called Dawes and Prescott to assist him in overpowering the two soldiers.

As Paul Revere went closer, four British officers with pistols ready to fire surprised and surrounded them. Paul Revere wrote that they said, "G-d d-n you stop. If you go an Inch further, you are a dead Man." Paul Revere and Dr. Samuel Prescott tried to force their way through the British soldiers but could not. The officers forced them into a pasture, and as Paul Revere put it, "swore if we did not turn into that pasture, they would blow our brains out."

This threat was not enough to hold Revere, Prescott, and Dawes. Once in the pasture, Prescott spurred his horse to the left and over a short stone wall and on to Concord. Revere turned his horse to the right "towards a Wood, at the bottom of the Pasture, intending, when I gained that, to jump my Horse and run afoot." When Revere reached the end of the pasture, six British officers were able to stop and surround him again. The soldiers had Paul Revere at gunpoint and ordered him to dismount from his horse. Dawes was able to sneak away when the soldiers went after Revere and Prescott.

Paul Revere was left alone in the hands of the British officers. The officer in command asked Revere where he came from and when he had left. He also asked, "Sir, may I crave your name?" Paul Revere answered, "Revere." The commanding officer asked, "Paul Revere?" and Revere answered, "Yes." The British officers that were waiting on the road knew of Paul Revere from his other express rides.

While being held by the soldiers, Revere told them that he knew what the British army was up to and that he had alarmed the whole countryside. With this news, Major Edward Mitchell, who was in charge of capturing express riders, came over to Paul Revere, put the pistol to his head, and asked more detailed questions about what Revere knew. Three other express riders, Solomon Brown, Jonathan Loring, and Elijah Sanderson, also had been captured. They had been held in the bushes by the road when Revere and his friends were stopped. After Paul Revere told him what he knew, the major decided to take the prisoners back to Lexington.

When the British soldiers and their four prisoners were outside of Lexington, they heard gunfire. Startled, Major Mitchell asked Paul Revere what the gunfire was for. Revere answered that it was "to alarm the country." The British officers, with Revere, were just coming into Lexington when they heard more gunfire. Major Mitchell decided that he and his troops should ride back to Cambridge and the advancing British army troops to tell them of the activity in Lexington. Revere was told to dismount his horse and give it to a sergeant so that he had a better horse for the ride. Paul Revere was set free but without a horse, and he headed back to Lexington once the British soldiers left.

Revere was lucky to have escaped his capture by the British. The alarm was successfully spread across the

Outside of the Buckman Tavern in Lexington, Massachusetts, the first shots of the American Revolution were fired between British soldiers and American militiamen in April 1775. The tavern still stands today in the center of Lexington.

countryside, as Revere went back to Lexington to find that Hancock and Adams had not left the house to get out of town. Revere returned and told them about his capture, which helped to convince Samuel Adams and John Hancock to leave for a safer location.

In the rush to leave town, John Hancock left a large trunk of his confidential papers at the Buckman Tavern. The papers were about the Revolutionary movement and could not fall into the hands of the British. Revere and John Lowell went to get the trunk as the rest of the Lexington militia gathered to meet the British on the Lexington Common. While Revere was getting the trunk, he saw the British coming very near, at a very fast pace. As Paul Revere was leaving town with the heavy trunk, he heard the first shots fired in the Battle of Lexington and Concord, the start of the Revolutionary War.

9. The Minutemen and the Battle of Lexington

The minutemen were gathered on the Lexington Common when the British army approached early on April 19. The British numbered about six hundred. They were under the command of Lieutenant Colonel Francis Smith and Major John Pitcairn. The troops rowed across the Charles River from Boston to Cambridge and began the march to Lexington.

On the march to Lexington, one British soldier noticed "a vast number of the Country Militia going over the Hill with their Arms to Lexington." The minutemen from towns around Lexington were running through the woods ahead of the British in an effort to beat them to Lexington and Concord. The minutemen knew the local landscape because they were all from the towns surrounding Lexington.

The militia in Lexington numbered fewer than one hundred men as the British army marched into town. When the leader of the Lexington militia, Captain John Parker, saw the British coming toward them, he ordered the minutemen to disperse so that the British could pass.

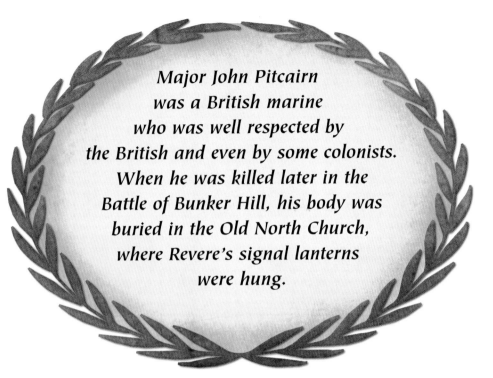

*Major John Pitcairn
was a British marine
who was well respected by
the British and even by some colonists.
When he was killed later in the
Battle of Bunker Hill, his body was
buried in the Old North Church,
where Revere's signal lanterns
were hung.*

Some minutemen got out of the way, but others did not hear the order and stayed in military formation. In the confusion, shots were fired, killing seven colonists and wounding one British soldier.

Nobody knows who fired the first shot on the Lexington Common. British and American accounts differ on the event. British Lieutenant John Barker recalled that the British soldiers were "keeping prepared against an attack tho' without intending to attack them, but on our coming near them they fired one or two shots, upon which our Men without any orders rushed in upon them, fired and put 'em to flight; several of them were killed."

Captain John Parker testified that on the approach of the British regulars, "I immediately ordered our Militia to disperse and not to fire. Immediately said Troops made their appearance, and rushed furiously, fired upon and killed eight of our party, without receiving any provocation therefor from us."

John Robbins was a member of the Lexington militia who was wounded in the first volley, or exchange of gunfire, at Lexington. He recalled that one of the British officers leading the charge of British soldiers called out, " 'Throw down your arms, ye villains, ye rebels.' " Robbins did not believe Captain Parker's men had fired first, but he remembers hearing another officer say, " 'Fire, by God, fire;' at which instant, being wounded, I fell."

Only two minutemen were killed on the line. The rest were killed while trying to leave. After the initial shots, the British soldiers went chasing after retreating minutemen until the officers were able to restore order. The British soldiers formed into their columns again and began the march to Concord.

The members of the Concord militia recorded that "about an hour after sunrise, we assembled on a hill near the meeting-house in Concord" after hearing the news of the shots fired at Lexington. When the British troops marched into Concord, the militia forces that had gathered retreated to a hill further out of town. The British regulars moved around the town, passed by the meetinghouse where the Concord

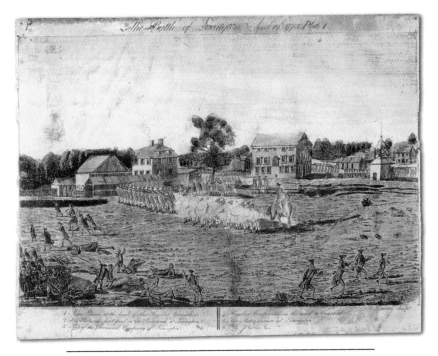

This painting of the Battle of Lexington was done by Amos Doolittle based on eyewitness accounts. He did four different plates documenting the running battles on April 19, 1775 at both Lexington and Concord. He labeled various things in the scene, including where Major Pitcairn stood and who fired first, based on the information from eyewitnesses.

militia had been, and onto the North Bridge.

Some Concord militiamen said, "We then seeing several fires in the Town, thought our houses were in danger, and immediately marched back toward said bridge and when we had got near the bridge they fired on our men." As the minutemen marched toward the bridge, it seems that a British soldier may have fired his gun by accident or against his orders. Several other nervous British soldiers then fired their muskets, and the Concord militia was ordered to fire on the British troops.

This was the first official order to fire on the British in the Revolutionary War. The Revolutionary leaders were very careful to point out that the British first fired on them and that the colonists were just responding in self-defense. Soon after the minutemen began to fire, the British regulars began to retreat.

The Battle of Lexington and Concord had not ended when the minutemen drove the British regulars from the North Bridge and back into Concord, though. It was just the beginning of a bloody series of battles that would rage all the way from Concord to just outside Boston. As minutemen continued to arrive from surrounding towns, the British officers decided to regroup

This photograph shows the portion of Battle Road looking east beyond Meriam's Corner. Imagine the colonial soldiers hiding behind the trees and stone walls, shooting at the British as they retreated down the road toward Boston.

and begin a march back to Boston. During the first part of the march from Concord back to Lexington, the British soldiers were fired upon by minutemen troops almost the entire time.

This retreat route from Concord to Lexington is known today as the Battle Road. In all of the battles during the day, many British soldiers were killed by minutemen who attacked from all angles. The minutemen fought as disciplined soldiers against the British army in the battles of Lexington and Concord. Most of the fighting by the minutemen was done from behind trees, low stone walls, hills, and houses along the roads from Concord to Boston. British soldiers had a hard time fighting back against the minutemen because they could not see what they were shooting.

When the British soldiers finally arrived back in Lexington, they were exhausted, beaten, and almost out of ammunition. There they were met by reinforcements from Boston led by Lord Hugh Earl Percy. When the British decided to move out from Lexington back to Boston, the minutemen did not take long to begin the constant attacks again.

Percy wrote in his report to General Gage, "We retired for 15 miles [24.1 km] under an incessant fire which like a moving circle surrounded and followed us." The minutemen from different towns each attacked from a different angle, most from strategic positions behind walls, trees, and in houses. The fighting continued in this manner until the British troops marched to Charlestown. Percy recalled later that the minutemen continued to attack "till we arrived at Charlestown, which road I chose to take, lest the rebels should have taken up the bridge at Cambridge."

Upon arriving on the open spaces and narrow entrance to Charlestown, the minutemen stopped the attack. The British soldiers, tired, without food, water, or much ammunition, waited to cross back to Boston from Charlestown. The Battle of Lexington and Concord was done, but the American Revolution was just beginning. Both the British and the colonists had suffered many losses, with many men dead or wounded on both sides. Nonetheless, the colonists had won the battle and had proved that they could stand up to the powerful British army.

After the battle, the Provincial Congress of Massachusetts collected the eyewitness accounts of the events. They sent these accounts to London as fast as they could to tell the colonists' side of the story to the people of England before General Gage could send in his report. The colonists wanted to show that the British army had attacked them and that they were protecting their liberty and property.

Right: This coffin broadside, "Bloody Butchery by the British Troops or the Runaway Fight of the Regulars," was used by Salem printer Ezekiel Russell to show the number of American casualties in the battle on April 19, 1775. At least six more editions were printed in the weeks after the battle, and Russell carefully added coffins as more soldiers died from their wounds. The broadside was used to raise public outrage in both America and Britain. It succeeded.

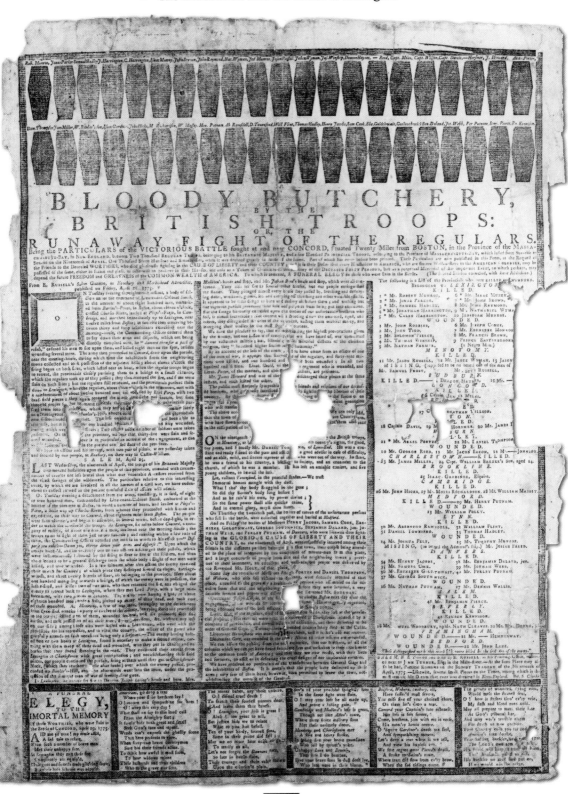

The colonial leaders also wanted to spread word of this event to all colonies and people. The Provincial Congress would have to raise an army and supplies for the fight against the British. The Battle of Lexington and Concord was an important event in convincing many that they had to defend their houses and property against the British.

After the Battle of Lexington and Concord, Paul Revere could not go back to his wife and family in Boston because the British army controlled the city. He met with the Provincial Congress in Cambridge, where Dr. Joseph Warren asked Revere to do the "out of doors work for the Committee." Revere probably played a large role in spreading the message of the Provincial Congress at the beginning of the Revolution. In May 1775, the Revere family moved to Watertown, Massachusetts. The Provincial Congress had hired Revere to engrave copper plates for the printing of money for the Massachusetts colony.

On June 17, 1775, the British army and the colonial militia fought the Battle of Bunker Hill, at Breed's Hill in Charlestown. This was a very bloody battle in which many British and colonial lives were lost. One of the most prominent leaders in Massachusetts, Dr. Joseph Warren, was killed in the fighting. Although he had been commissioned to become the first commander in chief of the Continental Army, he fought the battle as a private soldier. Warren's death was a big loss for the colonists. Paul Revere would name his son, born in 1777, Joseph Warren Revere in his friend's honor.

The British held off the attacks of the colonists at the Battle of Bunker Hill. One year later, though, the Continental Army surrounded Boston, and the British evacuated the city in March 1776. Revere and the other residents returned but remained on guard in case the British army tried to return.

Paul Revere's midnight ride and the other services he performed for the Provincial Congress were very important in the history of the Revolution. Revere's military record in the Revolutionary War was unremarkable compared to these other accomplishments. In 1776, Paul Revere was appointed a lieutenant colonel in the Massachusetts State Train of Artillery. He had wanted to be an officer in the Continental Army but was never appointed to a position. As a lieutenant colonel, he and his men were put in charge of Castle Island to guard Boston against the return of British troops.

The British never attempted to return to Boston, and Revere spent much of his time disciplining soldiers. The soldiers in Revere's command were probably more interested in rebuilding Boston after the British occupation of the city. In 1777, Revere and his state troops were called to bring British prisoners of war, captured in another battle, from Worcester back to Boston. Paul Revere's troops also marched to Rhode Island twice in failed attempts to move the British out of Newport. The second mission to Rhode Island was made in 1778, but Revere and his troops were not involved in any fighting.

In 1779, Paul Revere was named an artillery commander in a proposed attack on a British fort in Maine. The mission was known as the Penobscot Expedition. It was a failure for Paul Revere and the Continental troops. In a rare dark moment of Revere's life, he was censured and dismissed from the militia. In 1782, after many requests, Revere was cleared of any wrongdoing after a formal review of his actions.

10. Paul Revere: A Post-Revolutionary Businessman

After Paul Revere was dismissed from the military, his focus returned to his many business interests. Revere could turn again to his silversmith shop. The second period of silver production from Paul Revere's shop lasted from 1779 until just after 1800. The Revolutionary War had changed many things in Boston, including the success of Revere's shop.

Revere's records indicate that very few of his clients remained from before the Revolution. However, Boston experienced a period of prosperity after the war, so Paul Revere was able to gain new customers to replace the old ones who had left town. Although he did not have a larger number of customers, he made more money because new prosperity led people to buy more silver than they had bought before the war.

After the war, the products that came from Revere's silver shop were more standardized. For example, instead of customizing each cup or tea set, the same mold and design were used for several customers. Paul Revere did not personally make many of the silver

This tea pot was made by Paul Revere in 1789. It is marked with "•Revere" in a rectangle, and is engraved with the intials "MB" within a decorative crest. This tea pot is typical of the work Paul Revere was doing in his silvershop after the war.

goods that came from his shop after the Revolutionary War. His son, Paul Revere Jr., actually ran the business on a day-to-day basis, with Paul Revere managing. The development of more standardized silver production and the transfer of responsibilities to Paul Revere Jr. gave Paul Revere time to expand his silversmith shop and to explore other businesses.

The first new business that Revere opened after the war was a hardware store. He used the store to sell silver from his shop as well as goods that he imported from London. Revere had trouble getting goods from

London, and his interest in other businesses eventually led him to give up the hardware store.

By November 1788, Paul Revere had opened a foundry in the North End of Boston. A foundry is a factory that makes metal products from raw materials. Raw metals such as iron or copper are melted in large furnaces, or fires, and made into products both large and small. Paul Revere's shop was very close to many of the shipyards, so he was able to gain customers for his products quickly. Revere's foundry produced bolts, spikes, and nails for shipbuilders and others.

Besides these smaller items, Paul Revere also learned how to make bells for churches. Revere's first bell was cast in 1792 for the church that he attended. He soon made many more bells, some of

These are copper ship fittings manufactured around 1819 at Paul Revere's Copper Rolling Mill at Canton, Massachusetts, for the *USS New Hampshire*. The items are, clockwise from top left, a bolt, three spikes, and three nails. Photo is courtesy of the Paul Revere Memorial Association.

This is the trade card of Paul Revere and Son, engraved by Thomas Clarke between 1796 and 1803. This printing was done in 1944. A trade card like this would have been used to advertise their business.

which are still in New England churches today. Because bells were made of a mix of copper, tin, and other metals, Revere had to teach himself metallurgy, or the science of mixing metals.

In 1800, Paul Revere bought an old gunpowder mill in Canton, Massachusetts and began work in the final business of his career. After learning some metallurgy and researching the techniques of Europeans, Paul Revere learned how to roll copper. Supplying metal such as copper in large sheets was a big business. It was very important to the new American country.

No American had been able to roll copper into sheets successfully and profitably before Revere learned to do it in his mill. Sheets of copper were important to the new American navy. They needed it to cover the bottom of ships. The copper covering on the bottom of ships made them much faster and easier to maintain than wood. This innovation provided Revere with a very large customer: the new American government.

Paul Revere provided the copper for the bottom of the *USS Constitution* when it was repaired in the early 1800s. He also provided copper sheets for the dome of the Massachusetts State House. Revere's foundry, which was moved from Boston to Canton, also constructed boilerplates for the new steamships being developed by Robert Fulton.

Even while Revere worked on all of his new businesses, he remained politically active. Revere was still a member of the Masons and would remain active with them until the end of his life. He also was appointed to public office several times, once as a coroner and another time as the president of the board of health.

In the 1780s, Paul Revere was involved in the ratification of the newly created U.S. Constitution. Tradesmen and manufacturers met at the Green Dragon Tavern to vote on the new Constitution. The results were unanimously in favor of the new U.S. Constitution. Paul Revere then led the men through Boston to tell Samuel

Adams the result of the vote. This demonstration was said to have helped convince the Massachusetts leaders to ratify the federal Constitution.

Paul Revere also was involved in a new organization known as the Massachusetts Charitable Mechanics Association, which was made up of craftsmen like himself. Although there had been many clubs and associations in Boston, there never had been one that focused on craftsmen. The Massachusetts Charitable Mechanics Association was set up by craftsmen to support issues important to them, such as the system of apprenticeship and taxes on foreign products. It also was an organization that supported members going through hard times. It supplied them with money and food, among other things.

Paul Revere officially retired from all of his different business endeavors in 1811. He turned over the businesses to his son Joseph Warren Revere. Even with the official transfer of the business to Joseph Warren Revere, Paul Revere was still active in his businesses until the end of his life. With Paul Revere's guidance, Joseph Warren Revere was largely responsible for building the Revere Copper Company into a large New England industrial business.

Paul Revere's wife and companion of many years, Rachel, died in 1813. Revere's oldest son, Paul Revere Jr., also died in the same year. Paul Revere passed away a few years later on May 10, 1818. He was buried in

Boston, at a cemetery known as the Granary Burying Ground, next to Rachel and many of the other people in Paul Revere's past, such as Joseph Warren, John Hancock, and Samuel Adams.

One of the obituaries printed after Paul Revere's death appeared in the *Boston Intelligencer* on May 16, 1818. It read, in part, that Paul Revere was: "Cool in thought, ardent in action, he was well adapted to form plans and to carry them into successful execution, — both for the benefit of himself & the service of others. In the early scenes of our revolutionary drama, which were laid in this metropolis, as well as at a later period of its progress, his country found him one of her most zealous and active sons."

Paul Revere was remembered as an important citizen of Boston both for his service to the Revolutionary cause and for his talents as a silversmith and businessman. Paul Revere rarely boasted about his midnight ride, and he was not well-known around the country for his heroic role in pre-Revolutionary Boston at the time of his death.

Nevertheless, many people remember Paul Revere today only as the midnight rider of the American Revolution. This was the image created during the Civil War, more than forty years after Revere's death by the poet, Henry Wadsworth Longfellow. It is thought that Longfellow wrote the poem to show Paul Revere as a symbol of national unity. However, the poem ignored

This portrait of Paul Revere, and the facing one of his wife Rachel, was done by Gilbert Stuart in 1813. The portraits were commissioned by Paul Revere's son, Joseph Warren.

This portrait of Rachel Revere, and the facing one of Paul, was done by Gilbert Stuart in 1813. The portraits were completed only a few weeks before Rachel died.

Paul Revere's grave is in the Old Granary Burying Ground in Boston, Massachusetts, along with the graves of many other people who played a large role in shaping America.

the efforts of fellow patriots who also warned the countryside that the British were marching to Lexington and Concord. It also ignored the other impressive accomplishments of Paul Revere's life.

Paul Revere was not only the patriotic American who carried the warning to the countryside of the British army's march to Lexington and Concord. He was a talented silversmith, a responsible father, a patriotic citizen, and in his later years, a successful businessman. Revere's legacy is with us today in many ways. Revere silver is very valuable and is collected by many museums. Streets and towns across America today carry the name Revere in his honor. And some children across the country still learn Longfellow's poem that begins:

> *"Listen my children, and you shall hear*
> *Of the midnight ride of Paul Revere,*
> *On the eighteenth of April in Seventy-five,*
> *Hardly a man is now alive*
> *Who remembers that famous day and year."*

Timeline

1735	Paul Revere is baptized on January 1 in the North End of Boston, Massachusetts.
1754	Revere's father dies, and Paul Revere takes over the operation of the silvershop.
1756	Paul Revere joins the militia to fight in the French and Indian War.
1757	Sarah Orne and Paul Revere are married.
1758	Deborah, Paul Revere's first child, is born.
1760	The British government begins to enforce the Navigation Acts.
	Paul Revere joins the Masons.
1765	The Sons of Liberty begin meeting.
	The Stamp Act is passed by British Parliament.
1768	British forces sail into Boston on September 30.
1770	The Boston Massacre occurs on March 5.

1773   Sarah, Paul Revere's first wife, dies.
          Paul Revere marries Rachel Walker.

          The Boston Tea Party occurs on December 16.

          The first recorded express ride is made by
          Paul Revere on December 17.

1774   General Gage and the British government
          close Boston Harbor.

1775   Paul Revere rides to Concord on April 8,
          and to Lexington on April 15.

          The midnight ride of Paul Revere happens on
          the night of April 18 and morning of April 19.

          The Battle of Lexington and Concord
          occurs on April 19.

          The Battle of Bunker Hill occurs on June
          17. Joseph Warren is killed in the battle.

1776   British troops leave Boston for the final
          time in March.

          Paul Revere joins the Massachusetts State
          Artillery Train as a lieutenant colonel.

1779   The Penobscot Expedition ends in failure
          for the American troops and leads to Paul

Revere's dismissal from the militia.

1782	In a formal hearing, Paul Revere's name is cleared from any wrongdoing during the Penobscot Expedition.
1783	The Revolutionary War ends in American independence from Britain.
1788	Paul Revere opens a foundry.
1792	The first of many church bells is cast by Paul Revere.
1800	Paul Revere purchases an old mill outside of Boston in Canton to start a copper rolling business.
1811	Paul Revere officially retires from his various businesses.
1813	Rachel Revere and Paul Revere Jr. pass away.
1818	Paul Revere dies in Boston on May 10.

Glossary

ammunition (am-yoo-NIH-shun) Bullets and gunpowder used in firing a gun or cannon.

apprentice (uh-PREN-tis) A person learning a trade or craft from a skilled worker.

artillery (ar-TIH-lur-ee) A cannon, or other weapon for firing missiles such as cannonballs.

artisan (AR-tih-zuhn) An older term for a mechanic or craftsman. A person with a certain class of job, usually involving manual labor, and the production or repair of material items. Silversmiths, carpenters, shipbuilders, blacksmiths, and tailors would have been considered artisans.

broadside (BRAHD-side) A page, like a short newspaper, that gave current news of the day or advertisements.

charter (CHAR-tur) A constitution, or a written grant or guarantee of rights and priveleges of a city or state.

common (KAH-muhn) An open area in a town or city not owned by any one person, much like a park today.

depression (dih-PREH-shun) A period of low economic activity, slow growth, and high unemployment, or fewer jobs.

duty (DOO-tee) A tax or fee.

entrepreneur (ahn-truh-pruh-NUR) A businessperson who has started his or her own business.

express riders (ik-SPRES RY-durs) Men who spread news, alarms, and warnings between towns and cities in the colonies.

foundry (FOWN-dree) A factory with large furnaces, or fires, for melting and creating metal products.

immigrated (IH-muh-gray-tid) Having come into a country of which one is not a native to live permanently.

innovation (ih-nuh-VAY-shun) The creation of something new.

journeyman (JUHR-nee-muhn) A trained craftsman who does not own a shop but works for others.

lobsterback (LAHB-stur-bak) A slang term for a British soldier because of these soldiers' bright red uniform coats.

loyalist (LOY-uh-list) Colonists who were loyal to the British government and wanted to remain a colony of Britain. Also called Tories.

Masons (MAY-suhnz) Men who belong to a secret

society or brotherhood.

mechanic (mih-KA-nik) Another old term for an artisan or a craftsman. See artisan.

metallurgy (MEH-tuhl-uhr-jee) The science of knowing how to combine different metals for different products.

militia (muh-LIH-shuh) A part-time army of citizens who train and fight on behalf of their town or county.

minutemen (MIH-nuht-mehn) A specialized group of soldiers within a militia that were trained to be ready for battle at a moment's notice.

muster (MUHS-tuhr) To bring or call together, especially as a military group

Parliament (PAR-luh-mint) The law making, or legislative, body in Britain that is similar to the Congress in the United States.

pesthouse (PEST-hows) A location where people with contagious diseases were sent.

prosperity (prah-SPEHR-uh-tee) Good economic times, usually when many people have jobs and more money.

redcoat (RED-koht) A slang term for a British soldier because of these soldiers' bright red uniform coats.

regulars (REH-gyuh-luhrz) Men who are full-time

soldiers in an army.

rescind (rih-SIND) To withdraw, or take something back.

smuggling (SMUH-gling) Carrying cargo into or out of a country against the laws or without paying the taxes of that country.

Sons of Liberty (SUNZ UV LIH-ber-tee) A large group of revolutionaries, or Whigs, who protested the British government's taxes and unfair treatment before the Revolutionary War.

surtout (suhr-TOO) An old colonial word for a man's long overcoat.

Tory (TOR-ee) A colonist who was loyal to the British government and wanted to remain a colony of Britain, more commonly called a loyalist.

wharves (WORVZ) Large docks, or piers, where ships load and unload cargo and people.

whig (WIG) A colonist who believed that the British were treating the colonies unfairly and who wanted independence.

Additional Resources

To learn more about Paul Revere and the minutemen, check out these books and Web sites:

Books

Brandt, Keith. *Paul Revere, Son of Liberty*. Mahwah, New Jersey: Troll Associates, 1982.

Ford, Barbara. *Paul Revere: Rider for the Revolution*. Berkeley Heights, New Jersey: Enslow Publishers, 1997.

Fritz, Jean. *And Then What Happened, Paul Revere?* New York: PaperStar, 1973.

Grote, JoAnn A. *Paul Revere, American Patriot*. Edited by Arthur Schlesinger. New York: Chelsea House Publishers, 2000.

Leehey, Patrick. *What Was the Name of Paul Revere's Horse?: Twenty Questions about Paul Revere–Asked and Answered*. Boston: Paul Revere Memorial Association, 1997.

Web Sites

http://earlyamerica.com/review/winter96/massacre.html

www.nps.gov/mima/

www.paulreverehouse.org

Bibliography

Fischer, David Hackett. *Paul Revere's Ride*. New York: Oxford University Press, 1994.

Forbes, Esther. *Paul Revere and the World He Lived In*. Boston: Mariner Books, 1942.

Goss, Eldbridge Henry. *The Life of Colonel Paul Revere*. 2 vols. Boston: 1891.

Kehoe, Vincent J.R. (ed.). *We Were There!* 2 vols. Chelmsford, MA: 1975.

Morgan, Edmund (ed.). *Paul Revere's Three Accounts of His Famous Ride*. Boston: Massachusetts Historical Society, 2000.

Triber, Jayne E. *A True Republican—The Life of Paul Revere*. Amherst, MA: University of Massachusetts Press, 1998.

Zannieri, Nina et al. *Paul Revere—Artisan, Businessman and Patriot: The Man Behind the Myth*. Boston: Paul Revere Memorial Association, 1988.

Index

About the Author

Ryan P. Randolph is a freelance writer with an avid interest in history. Ryan has a Bachelor of Arts degree in both History and Political Science from Colgate University in Hamilton, New York. Ryan is also a member of the history honor society Phi Alpha Theta. He works in a financial consulting firm and lives with his wife in New York City.

About the Consultant

Patrick M. Leehey is the Research Director at the Paul Revere House. He has been on the professional staff for 15 years. His recent publications include *What Was the Name of Paul Revere's Horse?: Twenty Questions about Paul Revere-Asked and Answered*, and an essay, "Reconstructing Paul Revere: An Overview of his Ancestry, Life and Work" for the 1988 publication *Paul Revere— Artisan, Businessman, and Patriot: The Man Behind the Myth*. Patrick received his Master's degree in History and his Certificate of Museum Studies from Northeastern University.

Credits

Photo Credits

Pp. 4, 33, 40, 43, 90, 96, 97 Courtesy, Museum of Fine Arts, Boston. Reproduced with permission. © 2000 Museum of Fine Arts, Boston. All Rights Reserved; pp. 6, 23, 68-69 Courtesy of Map Division, The New York Public Library, Astor, Lenox and Tilden Foundations; pp. 11, 37, 85 Courtesy of American Antiquarian Society; p. 14 © Boston Atheneum; pp. 15 left, 22, 39 © CORBIS; p. 15 right © Galen Rowell/CORBIS; pp. 16, 91, 92 Collection, Paul Revere Memorial Association; pp. 18, 66 Images supplied by Commission of the Old North Church™; p. 20 Courtesy, Yale University Art Gallery, Gift of Susan Morse Hills; p. 21 Courtesy of Winterthur Museum; pp. 26, 46 © Boston Public Library/Rare Books Department. Courtesy of The Trustees; pp. 28, 30, 36, 42 Courtesy of Massachusetts Historical Society; p. 35 © Washington Lodge, A.F. & A.M., Lexington, MA; p. 45 © Yale Center for British Art, Paul Mellon Collection, USA/Photo Credit/Bridgeman Art Library.; p. 47 © A.K.G., Berlin/SuperStock; p. 48 © Lee Snider/CORBIS; p. 52 © Bettmann/CORBIS; p. 56 © Archive Photos; pp. 59, 98 © North Wind Pictures; p. 60 © SuperStock; p. 65 © Burstein Collection/CORBIS; p. 71 © Francis G. Mayer/CORBIS; p. 76 © Kevin Fleming/CORBIS; p. 81 © Arthur D'Arazien/SuperStock; p. 82 courtesy of the Concord Free Library.

Series Design

Laura Murawski

Layout Design

Corinne Jacob

Project Editor

Joanne Randolph